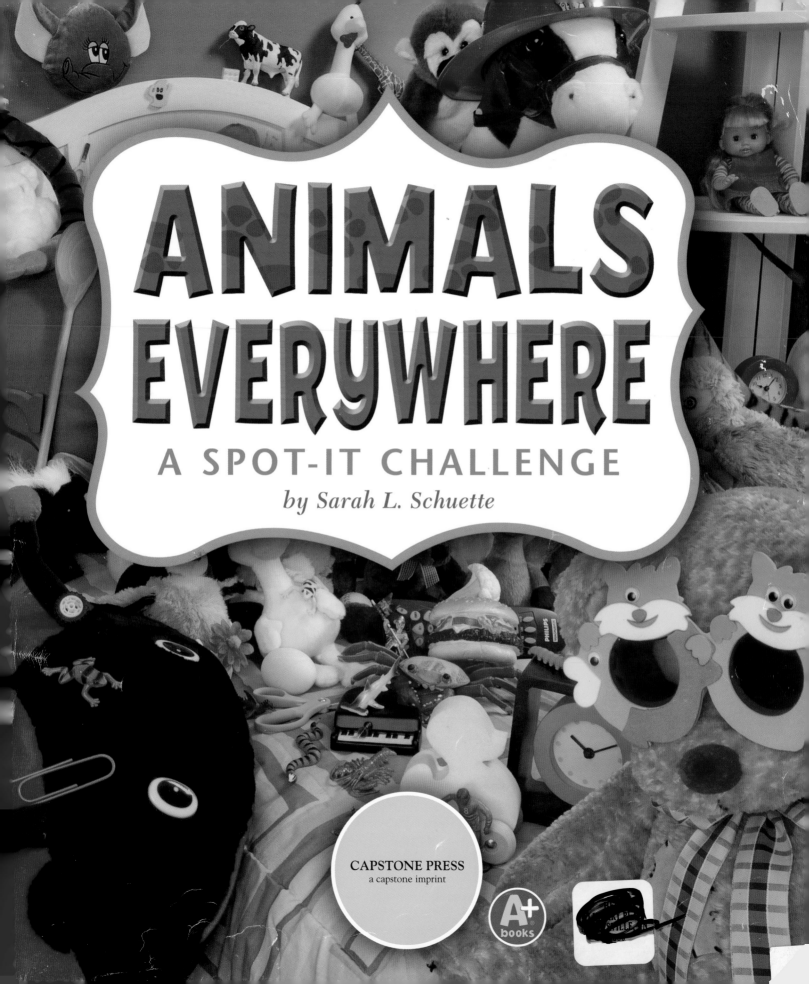

ANIMALS EVERYWHERE

A SPOT-IT CHALLENGE

by Sarah L. Schuette

CAPSTONE PRESS
a capstone imprint

A+ books

A+ Books are published by Capstone Press,
151 Good Counsel Drive, P.O. Box 669, Mankato, Minnesota 56002.
www.capstonepub.com

 Books published by Capstone Press are manufactured with paper
containing at least 10 percent post-consumer waste.

Library of Congress Cataloging-in-Publication Data
Schuette, Sarah L., 1976–
  Animals everywhere : a spot-it challenge / by Sarah L. Schuette.
      p. cm.—(A+ Books, spot it)
  Includes bibliographical references and index.
  Summary: "Simple text invites the reader to find items hidden in animal-themed
photographs"—Provided by publisher.
  ISBN 978-1-4296-4461-7 (library binding)
  1. Puzzles—Juvenile literature. I. Title. II. Series.
  GV1493.S316 2010
  793.73—dc22   2010018032

Credits

Jenny Marks, editor; Ted Williams, designer; Laura Manthe,
    production specialist; Sarah Schuette, photo stylist; Marcy Morin, photo scheduler

Photo Credits

all photos by Capstone Studio/Karon Dubke

Note to Parents, Teachers, and Librarians

Spot It is an interactive series that supports literacy development and reading enjoyment.
Readers utilize visual discrimination skills to find objects among fun-to-peruse photographs
with busy backgrounds. Readers also build vocabulary through thematic groupings, develop
visual memory ability through repeated readings, and improve strategic and associative
thinking skills by experimenting with different visual search methods.

The author dedicates this book to her friend Taylor Wendt of Belle Plaine, Minnesota.

Table of Contents

4

Don't Bug Me

Can you spot . . .

- a snail?
- a kidney bean?
- a killer whale?
- a princess gown?
- a sword?
- a birthday candle?

5

Think Spring

Can you spot . . .

- two checkers?
- a pineapple?
- a turtle?
- two helmets?
- a rooster?
- a carrot?

6

Wet & Wild

Can you spot . . .
- a blue paper clip?
- a nail clipper?
- a screwdriver?
- a comb?
- a heart?
- two ice cream cones?

9

Spot This

Can you spot . . .

- a gorilla?
- a milk jug?
- a toucan?
- an owl?
- six zebras?
- a police car?

Stuffed Up

Can you spot . . .

- a palm tree?
- a soccer ball?
- six clocks?
- two bones?
- a tennis racket?
- a horseshoe?

Safari

Can you spot . . .
- a battleship?
- a hotdog?
- an acorn?
- a kangaroo?
- a basket?
- a pirate?

Jungle Gym

Can you spot . . .

- a dustpan?
- two crocodiles?
- a lamp?
- a broom?
- a stingray?
- a unicorn?

Ssss

Can you spot . . .

- a whistle?
- a rubber ducky?
- two butterflies?
- a globe?
- a roller skate?
- a toothbrush?

19

Arctic Blast

Can you spot . . .
- a UFO?
- a mouse?
- a pretzel?
- a dove?
- two daisies?
- two slices of bread?

21

Get a Pet!

Can you spot . . .

- a silver bone?
- an elephant?
- an igloo?
- a football?
- a beetle?
- two rabbits?

Dino-mite

Can you spot . . .

- a humpback whale?
- a clover?
- six macaroni noodles?
- a walrus?
- two matchsticks?
- a cowboy boot?

Pig Pile

Can you spot . . .
- a pink high heel?
- a watering can?
- a fence?
- a plastic bandage?
- a hammer?
- a flamingo?

Spot Even More!

Don't Bug Me

5

Now try to find a train engine, a fire extinguisher, a bathtub, a smiley face, and a single tire.

Think Spring

6

Look for a castle, two pencils, a seashell, a flip flop, and a watermelon slice.

Wet & Wild

9

See if you can spot a bowling pin, a present, a cookie cutter, a key, and two divers.

Spot This

10

See if you can find two polar bears, a guinea pig, a skeleton, a helicopter, and two snowflakes.

Stuffed Up

13

Look for a wizard, a fall leaf, a sea star, a raccoon, a remote control, and a bell.

Safari

14

Try to spot a trumpet, a baseball glove, a nest, two teddy bears, and five eggs.

Jungle Gym

This time find a gnome, a jackhammer, two maracas, a snowman, and an ice cream scoop.

Ssss

See if you can find a football player, three pea pods, a stick bug, a sailboat, and a ladybug.

Arctic Blast

Find a toaster, a computer, a green pair of goggles, a jogger, and a ghost.

Get a Pet!

Take another look to find a dragonfly, two frogs, two dice, a robot, a teepee, and a tennis ball.

Dino-mite

Now spot a bunch of grapes, a mitten, a swan, a pine cone, a cannon, and three soda cans.

Pig Pile

Try to find a cupcake, a thimble, a snake, a wire whisk, and the letter "Y".

Extreme Spot-It Challenge

Just can't get enough Spot-It action? Here's an extra animal-fun challenge. Try to spot:

- a crown
- a bobber
- an eagle
- a pony
- a knight's shield
- a piano
- a Dalmatian
- an eraser
- an anchor
- the Statue of Liberty
- a moon
- a cake
- three baseballs
- a hamburger
- a traffic cone
- a mushroom
- a light bulb

Read More

Bruning, Matt. *Zoo Picture Puzzles.* Look, Look Again. Mankato, Minn.: Capstone Press, 2010.

Harbo, Christopher L. *What's That Shadow?: A Photo Riddle Book.* Nature Riddles. Mankato, Minn.: Capstone Press, 2010.

Marzollo, Jean. *I Spy an Egg in a Nest.* Scholastic Reader. New York: Cartwheel Books, 2011.

Internet Sites

FactHound offers a safe, fun way to find Internet sites related to this book. All of the sites on FactHound have been researched by our staff.

Here's all you do:

Visit *www.facthound.com*

Type in this code: **9781429644617**